Woman of March

poems by

Yumiko Tsumura

Finishing Line Press
Georgetown, Kentucky

Woman of March

ACKNOWLEDGMENTS

The author gratefully acknowledges the following publications in which some of
these poems first appeared, sometimes with slight modifications.

*Kyoto Journal, Poetry Kanto, Manoa, Eastlit,
Wisconsin Review, Cancer Poetry Project 2,
Rogues's Gallery, The Infidel, Daybreak,
Moon Rabitt Review, Hidaka News,
Poetry Review Tampa, Sou'wester,
Pyramid, Ab Intra, Quixote, Intrepid,
Cronopius, road apple review, Word,
Ann Arbor Review, The Poetry Bag,
South & West, The Lampeter Muse.*

Publisher: Leah Maines

Editor: Christen Kincaid

Cover Art: Yumiko Tsumura

Author Photo: Paul Mathews

Cover Design: Paul Mathews

Printed in the USA on acid-free paper.
Order online: www.finishinglinepress.com
            also available on amazon.com

Author inquiries and mail orders:
Finishing Line Press
P. O. Box 1626
Georgetown, Kentucky 40324
U. S. A.

Table of Contents

To Junko (純子)

My Pacific War on the Hidaka Plain
(on my memory wall)

When I was six years old
I ate rice porridge and potato vines
occasionally broiled locusts
and chewed sugar cane
all the flowers were gone
I practiced writing characters
on the edge of newspapers
filled with war propaganda
under a dim light
the spirit coming out of a radio
was explosive

I marched to the whistle
a long footpath between rice paddies
to the school
lined up with village children
a cotton helmet on
when I heard the siren
B-29's were coming, I ran
to hide my little body
in the bamboo bush
or put myself into a gunny sack
and laid down on the dirt
to play opossum
when we arrived safe
at the school playground
we first turned our heads
to the east and made a profound
bow to the monument
kami was enshrined
in the morning sun
after Long Live the Emperor

we squatted and weeded
under the scorching sun
my head was fainting white

At night I saw
the smoky lit red sky
in the east on the other side of the mountain
"Osaka got it!
Water to a burning stone"
I learned the name of
the old city

Dark clouds were approaching
the Hidaka Plain

Just then August 15, 1945
the deploring voice of the Emperor
filled the room
the blank faces of adults
the wondering eyes of children
all was
in a still time

And then
there was the sound of the waves
of the Pacific Ocean

Having escaped into
life, I saw
my father's large magnanimous hands
my mother's enduring hands
I was glorious
with the thought of
a white blank
sheet of paper to write
my name

Today Again

I didn't want
a day to start
with a coffee spoon.

I hurried to
the beach through a street
busy with morning.

On cool sand
between pine trees
and sea
my feet looked for
the beginning of day.

In the distance
fishermen drag a seine,
revolve with sand.

A woman's wet shoe
moves into
the light.

The Sun Is Setting

I slip out from my parents
and sit beside the fence.
Looking at the light falling
on my toes, I undo
the bundle of my secrets.
Wind and leaves are welcome.
Soil is fresh now.
Each of my secrets flies up
and cries out loud.
My bones are stretched into the light.
This spot stands still.
I wish I could send this
bundle with the setting sun.
Mother's call moves my feet
into the darkness of the house.

The Kitchen

When I hear father
yelling, I hurry to
the kitchen
and do the dishes
quickly.

Mother's feet tug
at the floor.
Her hand gropes for
a place
in her apron.
At the tip
of her chin
a dream
burns quietly.

I put the heavy
dishes away
carefully
for tomorrow.

Woman of Straw

"When a woman marries she lives
in shadows cast
by a tree's happiness."

Her legs cool in the kitchen,
her head turns toward
her husband at his study.
She pours him tea with smiles.
She lives through
the turning of pages.

She liked college. Plato died.
She prepared her husband's favorite
fish. Days went by like paper.

A breeze touches her
face turning towards an empty platter.

The Night of Junko's Birth
(for Motoi)

September is the month of
typhoons in the island country Japan
but it was a calm warm night
on Kii peninsula when you were pulled out of
my injured body with broken bones and cracked pelvis
by the old doctor's hands with a pair of forceps
because the umbilical cord that yoked us was short

in spite of the car accident in the Cascade Mountains
that took your father's life and spared us
you came to this earth without even a scar
with all your faculties intact

embraced by the wonder of life
as I lay side by side with you
the pain and fear faded

it was plenty bright with
less than a full moon
I thanked even pebbles

The Encounter
(for Sam)

it was not
that you turned me around
or just pushed me to open
just facing you

something free and naked
as laughter
leaped into me
through the pores of my skin

and dug me up
I had been buried alive
in the desert of
discipline

Junko

You were four years old
when you came into our hangover bed
between me and my lover
and sang loudly
    "a rose opens, a red rose opens, in our lonely garden"
looking at the book upside down

You were four years old
when we took you to an American restaurant in Kobe
You couldn't eat hard bread
I didn't know your front teeth were gone

You were four years old
when I saw your gaze go vacant
from the train window
and your waving hand stop

You know your grandparents footfalls
You know what stone is your father
You know me by the name "Mama" or "America"

Mold in August

sunflowers open in the light
swelling clouds rise
the river calls people

a small mold
crawls somewhere in my body
day breaks in a room
of sunlight and electricity

two hornets inspect
a gauze window
young as I am
my flesh stings

In My Sleep

fatigue spreads
her wings
and holds me
in her beak
and takes me to the
other side of me

I am awake
in my sleep
weaving through
the myriad islands
of memory, fear and desire

and float up
into the light
like a submarine
breaking the surface
of day

The Memory

lying down in the dark
I descend my ladder
and meet my skeleton
it is not
wet any more
the defenseless skeleton

while I have built
my ladder this high,
its blood has faded
under the sun

I drink saliva
and hear my throat
sing in the dark

Rain

What I want to be
is raining softly.
The river has more water.
The rice plants are growing.
Do you hear the music
of the rain?
I want to die
as the rain leaves off.

Portrait of an Afternoon

on the concrete square
women are talking terribly fast
as if a war were to hit
this town

on the concrete square
men are walking terribly quick
as if a bomb were to hit
this town

> the windows of high buildings are closed
> the fountain throws water into the autumn sky
> looking for something green

the sun does not reach
the veins of this town

In January

As I came out of
the concrete block house
a few red
leaves on a dark bough
aroused
my eyes

Tonight
I think of the fossil-like
old
man's mind
flashing
on his work

In a Box

My dream was a noisy
place I
had a cast
on my nerves

This early
in the morning

        men hammering
        construction job
        bulldozer swagger
        dandelions bloom
        the shade of buildings

I read of the world

        of people bathing in the river
        of corpses

And yet I think of

        a baby being born somewhere

This early
in the morning
I am a meteorite

My Orbit

Though the red quince blooms in my garden
I go out
with a fist in my heart
to

                  The morning city where the sun
                        breaks on armored skin
                  The midday city where polished
                        leather and nails shine
                  The night city where people come and go
                        like funeral cars in dreams
                        to purchase rest

In the city
the forest of muffled minds
tries to escape the shadows
of fear

Though the red quince blooms in my garden
I go out
with a fist in my heart
to

                  The city where there is no room
                  for a password
I am
        an owl

                  that cannot return to the woods
                  I search for a word
                  that reaches
                  my core

On a Clear Autumn Day

the old man sat
on the roadside granite
all morning
all afternoon
looking at his green
mansion being torn down
under the name of
city planning

surrendering to
his misfortune
quietly anguishing
to the tip of his nails
he held in his hand
one fir cone
left by the claw
of the bulldozer

The Buddhist Priest

Snow was falling
on the temple
the voice reading sutra
cutting the night
incense floats
in the room
my thought turned to
the dead.

The priest came in
and gave me a red
camellia. Flakes of
snow on petals.
His feet moved quietly
into the darkness.

A Mountain Is There

Today again
the young men died
believing in
mountain climbing

My aunt gave me
a basket of oranges
she grows
love on a mountain

Oh, This Is

lovely
to wake up
in the house, birds are conversing out in the garden
just like mother and father used to do
early summer morning
walking to the kitchen
around the atrium
blossoms of peace lilies smile
at my footsteps
the gold fish come out from under the rocks
red ones, orange ones
so does my love out of his study
to welcome me
into the
day

A Guest

Opening the curtain
this early morning
I saw a face
a crimson hibiscus
looking in
I bowed
"Good morning"

A Magnolia Experience

I

after winter rains
seep down
the soil softens,
clenched green buds
out on the bare bough

as the water warms
to my skin the life inside
pushes to open
three layered petals one
by one

stretching to the sky
with all your might
a gentle crimson
I salute your
sovereignty

II

a gentle spring
rain flutters you down
leaving the thumb-sized
green hearts on the branch
a rich quietness

then the small leaves
emerge in
dazzling force
the withering hearts give
way to the full
young green
I wash my eyes
in the May light

III

there is some
time, some time

come, birds
all birds
there is time

before
we dance
with sunset-color leaves
in autumn
wind

Hanging On

Captured inside
the helplessness of the disease
of a loved one

1

I could not go into the sun but
brought inside
a few small white roses from the fence
staying near them
I hung on

2

I unplugged the telephone
closed the curtains
lived in dim light, but
I went to the market
and a friend was calling me
My winter Camellia inside
opened its red petals, one, two, three
as I heard my name

3

I had to keep moving forward
I walked into my classroom
the room was warm
with orange yellow light
I became a blossom
Students came
to drink my nectar

He Came to Say Goodbye to Me

A tree doctor told me
this cherry tree has
a disease, it is getting rotten
from within the roots

Another doctor in Japan
found gangrene in my father's leg

(a creeping decay inside
such dignity and elegance)

The biggest branch died first

My father's left leg was amputated

One year later at the end
of January the cherry blossomed
in a flickering burst
one last time
looking at me in the chilled air
outside my window

(such an extra-ordinary visit)

At night in my sleep
the spirit of the cherry
wrapped a warm arm
around my neck

Across the Pacific
in a hospital room in Gobo
just like gentle rain ends
quietly alone
my father took off
on another journey

The Visit

This morning
maybe because I watered the garden
filled the bird bath, weeded and removed
the dead flowers
a bird came to my garden
talking in a familiar voice

I opened the window
and burst into "Where is
my mother? Did you bring
my mother?"

Wrinkles

my mother was
a tiny thin woman
with big bones, strong hands
and agile legs
always working from dawn to dusk
talking to herself laughing
she loved the wrinkles on her forehead
saying they are her fortune

one spring day in the village of Takara
when her sweet pea field
blossomed soft-pink
she came to tell me
with running sweat from weeding
"a white butterfly came to visit"

she was a woman content
even in her wrinkles

when lost and tired
I wish I could crawl
in between her soft
wrinkles and
sleep

California Poppy

When the Pacific War began
my California born mother was
ostracized in the village
and after the war ended
she could not share her
childhood memories, the tacit bondage
with the people in the remote
town called Gobo

She kept her hands and knees
engaged from dawn to dusk

When the air softened in peace
and English became a fashion
she started growing a western
flower (I didn't know the name
or where she got the seeds)
and started bubbling in sparkles of
her little school days with
black, brown and white friends
just then my appetite
bigger than Gobo was born

She was moved from her native continent
to a small island in the Pacific for life
I moved, by my choice, from Gobo
all the way to this new haven
still so bewildered
but never miss seeing
this wild, sun-colored flower

with satiny petals and blue green leaves
whose blooms close at night called
California Poppy

The Blessing

July 7th is *tanabata*
the romantic star
festival day

crossing the heavenly river
Junko and Igor
exchanged vows

in white silence
the color of the day
beams and beckons

among the fragrance
of roses, lily of the valley,
stephanotis and glossy green
the embracing eyes of people
from East and West celebrating
the poignant union
of the two musicians

tasting
the nectar of
the shining day

Into a New Century
(for Kazuko Shiraishi)

I did not see the last
sunset of the 20th century
on this continent but
I called the poet of
"burning meditation"
who lives across the Pacific
in mammoth Tokyo
on the crowded
islands in the eastern sea

Listening to her open
enormous energy
I saw the first
sunrise before the new
year began

and waking up in Palo Alto
on the cold morning I bathed
my eyes with tiny clear
white blossoms of Jade plants
in the first light of
the New Century

Eiko's Gift

your calls across the Pacific
always
brought a refreshing
taste of lemon sherbet
to my day

when we were together
our time had the
color and tender
fragrance of
a yellow rose
with your neat
and sweet
elegance

A Birthday Gift
(for Igor)

Getting past the hard
knots, bamboo
grows straight
upward to the sky

With this humble
bamboo spoon
scoop two heaps
of this powdered tea
from old Kyoto

Pour boiling water
a fourth of the bowl
and whisk until
you see foam

A sip will cleanse
your senses
and give you
a moment of oneness
with nature
in this time of war

and you will practice
your cello
with a beginner's mind
again

My Room

a solid delta
in rainbow color
where the two rivers from
the East and the West
meet

1

A card came
from Kyoto.
An abstract sculpture
white alabaster
of standing rock melting
into a bigger
gentle egg like being
radiating
harmony peace romance
Isamu Noguchi
The Kiss 1945

2

A card came
from Kyoto.
A powerful mastered motion of an ink brush
on a gentle mulberry paper
expressing the ideograph
Stone Garden 5.19.1992
the fluidity of an enlightened being

3

A card came
from Kamakura.
Cherry Tree at Daigoji Temple
Togyu Okumura 1972

the misty silver pink
a romance with the tree

4

A card came
from Woodside, California.
to wish me a happy Spring
a proud woman with
a medallion in pink blue brown
striding to a
direction, not a
phantom at dawn

5

A card came
from New York.
On a young green hill
her little house
and my big house are
connected
by a red heart-shaped
telephone line
"Mother, even though
we're far apart"

6

A card came
from Blue Springs, Missouri
A deep green window
frame in three partitions
each filled
with a golden letter
J O Y

superposed on
fading brown leaves

7

A card came from Varazdin
the old capital of Croatia
A birthday wish in naive art
many chains of small round clouds
float in the wine pink sky
over a village of six small houses
each a different shape with two windows
they look like faces
gazing at the young green field
after a good long sleep
Spring has come

8

A card came
from Montmartre, Paris
A happy new year wish
Catherine Poire's oil painting of
Sacre Coeur in red orange yellow
the colors of her love for
the people who gather there
from all over the globe

9

And
there is one more,
an old card
The village called Takara
between orange mountains and a pine beach
white waves of the Pacific Ocean

washing the pebbles
Every night I trust
my love-lit lantern
to the waves

After Your Untimely Departure

Eiko,
I lament
not coming to say
thank you
for your gift of
friendship
because you left me too soon

This year when I take a walk
in crisp air of May
at dawn
I see you in the dainty
petals of hydrangeas
in melancholy blue

I wonder if they will turn
pink next May
after more rendezvous
in my dreams
with you

Care Partner

Always with our wings spread
we flew high and wide
together in a trance with
simple and profound
timelessness until
one of our wings snapped
My love's cancer spread its claws
and engulfed us in darkness

We crawl on the path
of radiation and chemo drugs
nights and days, I scream
into a pillow
spitting phlegm out
of my brain
At night the black hole is visible

In the morning white light bends on my skin
The red maple leaves have fallen with gusts and rain
Winter is near
I think of my brother and sister across the Pacific
I think of my daughter across this continent
My dead parents are looking at me through pictures
my father with Buddha's benevolence
my mother with an enduring smile

As though they answered
there was a gentle knock at the door
A friend brought me
cooked seaweed and taro potatoes

My tongue dove deep
into my roots in the village
I devoured the memories of
the sea and the soil

Even with broken wings, we will
soar again
together

The Permanence

it was into August
your birth month
when your oncologist told you
"you have come to
the end of your life,
so every morning when you wake up
do the most important first"
the doctor gave us "a group hug"
before parting

that day
after coming home numb
we laid ourselves down flat on the floor
side by side holding each other's hands
in the brilliant light of August
with a cool breeze from the garden on our faces
listening to the silence
in the pulse of time

our eyes went to Miro's "The Pygmies Under the Blue Moon"
the two pygmies playing with some preoccupation
the blue moon in motion
together we tasted
the kernel and
melted

outside the picture window
a humming bird came to
the tiny red flowers of Salvia
we grew in our garden

You and Me

> *"What we call the beginning is often the end*
> *And to make an end is to make a beginning."*
> —T.S. Eliot, Four Quartets

you wrote to me
from your death bed
"what you now begin is a new us"

the cancer came
between us and
ended your life
we could not wave
a magic wand

you surrendered to
the ebb tide of your life
bigger than we are
with magnanimous grace
and entered the infinite
quietness

on Thanksgiving Day
I saw you lying in repose on a wooden board
covered in a white flannel blanket
just as you were born

I surrender to
the beginning of
"a new us"
you in the other world
me in this world

your river will
meet my river
in the Pacific Ocean
one day
you and I
will have a whirl
dance

The Red Peonies

one day in spring
after strolling the marina in San Francisco
you bought me
a Chagall's lithograph
"Bouquet of Peonies"
spending all our savings

it took us back to the spring in the village
on the small island country in the Eastern sea
where the fire of our life was lit

we hung it on the wall of our bedroom
I often found myself awake before dawn
intensely looking at the red peonies in the dark
in our warm bed

now in my solitary bed
it embraces me
with the strong and tender
arms that my body
remembers

"A New Us"

you wrote every day
journals of your thoughts
poems and stories
throughout our forty years
and my hands were tied up
with the immediate

only occasionally peeping into
your kingdom of imagination
letting my urge to share
your most important came second
during your earth time

now in this infinite
quietness I go gentle
into your treasure room
to read, hear and see
each drop of your life
living inside you
becoming your eye

even in my dark hours
we are
growing together

A Tender Hand

unable to surrender
to the loss
struggling to get through
one dawn to another
this Saturday morning I let
this May verdure move my feet out to
the farmer's market I have missed
a few springs

through the veil of my mourning
I watched the people-fest
the sound of joyful bubbling, sparkles and banjo music
the colors of enticing fruit, vegetables and flowers
the rich yolk of human life, enjoying the gifts nature gives
until I saw an apparition of
a familiar face in the crowd
I shouted "Eva"
as though I found a treasures I left behind
it broke through the veil and made a hole

Eva said
"this is our memorial for Sam
under the oak tree and open sky"
after a warm hug

the pulse of life
is beginning to come in
through this small hole
with a tender hand

Today a Fairy Came and

gave a bouquet of white roses to
my husband's altar and

a pair of purple sandals for my feet and
lifted me up into
a space where there is only now

the August light so poignant to my skin
I could even live with flying termites

the rouge clouds of dream floating
in the summer sky

Like a White Egret in June
(for Paul)

Returning from the journey
seeing off the dead
to the woods of the souls
in the Buddha country
on the other side of the river

I saw something moving in dim light
as though you were waiting for me
on this side of the river
in the Moonlight Sonata

You appeared from the land of wonder

Your solid wings
have taken me to a new
field, I taste the sweetness
of light in green air
I am giggling
again

The Way

you have explored
long enough
and came to it

and you moved
in a straight line
without hesitation

like the line of footprints
of a squirrel on snow
finding an acorn

wondrous
with passion
and grace

An Autumn Joy

our neighbors offered to share
persimmons from their tree,
the Fall gifts from nature

remembering the old way
I peeled and skewered them with bamboo spits
and hung them in a cold room
hoping the tannin turns sweet
ready for the new year

the heart-shaped persimmons
lit our Autumn days,
bright lanterns

A March Episode

"Hello, this is Hella Berg . . .
(a familiar voice, long forgotten
reaching the corner of my flickering mind)
are you Yumiko?"

"Yes, I am."
remembering her beaming face with the joy of teaching.

"You appeared in my dream last night and
I was up from four looking for your telephone number."

"I am glad you found my footprint,
are you still at the same house?"

"Yes, but I have nothing to do now, I don't have any disease
but have no energy and I can't entertain anymore. I sit in the shade
of the oak tree in my garden, I am 88, so it's OK if I die tomorrow."

She had a fire burning for a long time, teaching German and Japanese.
Now her life and death meet face to face.
Her voice says she wants to go
just like a bird flies off a cliff.

"Yumiko, don't give up teaching, it is such a noble profession."

Our sleeves touched
in our walks
of life.

Once There Was

Fragrance of roses
in this shining wind of May
has brought that brilliant
room of mirth back

the art of tea bowl from Kyoto
golden pink roses in the crystal vase from Varazdin
black forest gateau with
whipped cream, maraschino cherries and chocolate shavings
Junko playing piano and Igor playing cello

There was that time
our life had grown sweet as
a caress

It is nice to meet them now
in my dreams

The Path Not Swept Away

(for the surviving victims of the 11-Mar-2011 Tsunami)

in the time of expecting a divine
visitation of cherry blossoms
on the islands of Japan

the bottom of the Pacific near the northeast coast
opened a behemoth mouth and
swallowed the villages and towns

and the world watched smoke
from the Nukes
trembling in memory of black
rain after the Pacific War

the claw marks coming live
out of the screen nights and days
tell our senses
the one is the all
and the all is the one

the dead shall die no more
after a short sleep they return to
a new you
and stay with you
and you breathe and grow
together

a warm blanket of
close-knit kinship is your
safety net

and soon
from the same sea that took
your loved ones and your life's treasures
you will enjoy
seaweed and fish
again

At a Summer's End

today a long time Japanese friend
answered my telephone call
it was a voice of a man who has renounced the world
a burnt-out combatant on this American continent
giving care for his stroke suffering wife
for over a decade
he said she has become an enemy

as though harnessing light from a needle point
in a dark bleak place
he confessed pain from his deep well
in his native language saying
some days he chooses not to go to see her
and listens to
opera all day long

it is not distant daughters, nor a big house and savings
that gives him solace
his love for opera is his sole companion

however shredded
he will not brake

The Bird
(for Michiko)

inspired by a dream of America
in the aftermath of the Pacific War
you and I came out of the Japanese islands
to pursue the literature
of this continent

we had an enduring encounter
when our narrow bumpy paths crossed
a little bird flew between us
even though we were treasuring it dearly
each of us had moved on
to another pursuit

surviving the winds and waves of life
having sipped the nectar
of a long silence
the bird with stronger wings
carried your message
from thousands of miles away

leaping time and space
the embrace of our reunion
in profound silence
had the divine purity
of cherry blossoms

it will keep flying between us
our "song of now"
with delicious laughter
resonates on this
continent making our
transient life
boundless

Slice of Heaven

having secured
seaweed, and fermented beans
for my native pallet
at a market

driving under
arched elm trees
in morning rays through leaves

listening to the Dvorak Cello Concerto
bathing my soul in
the lyrical melody of
profound pathos
and longing for infinite
earth time

returning home to
growing plums and eggplants
ripening in purple,
pink begonias smiling
sparrows singing

a yellow butterfly fluttering by
a magical visit
ahhh!

Magical Moments on an Expedition to Poland

"We must love one another or die" —*W. H. Auden*

70 years after the end of World War II
I paid homage with a tour group to
Westerplatte in Gdansk on the Baltic Sea
treading the ground the Nazis invaded
September 1, 1939, the beginning of World War II
my stomach feeling a chill
I moved on to the city center
my eyes seeing a fairly tale
Gothic buildings in vibrant colors
castle-like towers and archways

in and out of Baltic amber shops
translucent golden-brown hues
the warmth of amber from prehistoric times
traveling through my body

just then, a dainty lady in our group
appeared in front of me on the cobblestones
speaking to me with thorns in her voice
she was insulted by a sales person
for taking too much time choosing amber for her friends
while she spent only fifteen minutes
her indignation reached my core
and we got connected
her name is Sakul
she is from the kingdom of Thailand

the next morning after walking through Auschwitz
Sakul was pale with loss of sleep
I woke up exhausted with nightmares

> an abyss of terror and scream
> with no way out for the condemned
> the eyeballs, the hair, the teeth, the cups and shoes
> reaching out from the abyss
> scorched naked
> bodies fuming forever

the television was showing Germany
welcoming waves of refugees from Syria

in Krakow, visiting Schindler's gloomy
factory with military pots and pans
I had an urge to dine with cheerful music
and Polka dancers like Polish dolls

in Torun, the medieval town
the birthplace of Copernicus
Sakul gave me a bag of gingerbread
made since the Middle Ages in the city
I tasted the artisan's pride

in Poznan, I had the delight of a simple lunch
dill sprinkled potatoes with cottage cheese
from the vast and fertile farmland
their recipes became new friends
on the dinner table at home

in Malbork, walking through the awe inspiring
brick Castle of the Teutonic Order
I was possessed by the presence
of the stoic Knights
who lived in the medieval fortress

at last, in Warsaw, after a Chopin concert
as we walked through evening streets
Sakul held my hand tight
with her delicate and strong hand
to protect me from pickpockets
her tender passion
flowed into me
bringing good luck to my life
as though a radiant ladybug
landed on me

In the Realm of Earth

"Even if I knew that tomorrow the world would go to pieces,
I would still plant an apple tree" —*Martin Luther*

in March I dug
a patch of yard
and made a rich bed
for the Japanese
cucumber plants
believing in them
I planted each
with love

a humble amount of water
and unfailing sunshine helped them
grow taller than my height
and clear yellow flowers brought
lustrous green gifts
with a nostalgic flavor
throughout summer heat

in September I had to leave them
when I went on
an expedition to Poland
they were waiting for my return
and gave me joyful company
on the dinner table

but in the tender light of October
they were slowly going down
at last, late in the month
I pulled out the plants
thanking them for visiting and giving me
special summer delight

touching and tapping
the soil, my dear friend
with bare hands
my body felt
peace

after seeing them off
I watched the autumn clouds
pass by

Crossing a Night

I closed my eyes
to shut out the light and the noise
of a bumpy day
and tried to count sheep
as my western doctor said
it did not take me
to a sleep land

I see the miscellanies
standing with must-placards
in the square of my mind
then faces of loved ones, images from music
and words of poets
appear and make a symphony
night flowers bloom
in the blue square

after joys of the night
I take myself back to the quiet
beach to sit
with mother and father
to watch the evening sun
slowly setting
over the horizon of the Pacific
the warmth of pebbles
the sound of waves
as darkness
engulfs me

A November Thought

everything is transparent
in this tender light of November
most of my beloved ones are dead
but more alive in my universe
and beckon me to my roots

born in an old house in a village between mountains and ocean
in the Hidaka plains that survived bombs and the hunger of war
I used to ride a bike early mornings through the pine forest
and walk barefoot on the beach sand wondering
what is beyond the horizon

I am an amalgam of Samurai father and California born mother
my parents' love sent my aspiration-kite flying away high to the west
across the Pacific to the American continent
I live in a space between the two extremes
always hearing the two voices

over half a century now
the world is connected with one fingertip
moving faster and surrounded by fears of bombs again
but I see the surviving children smiling arm in arm
walking through heaps of rubble to school
whether hit by tsunami or bomb
light of hope travels faster than darkness

at night
I drink loquat tea and take western medicine
I lie down in my mother's flannel kimono
on a futon in a small room with moonlight
listening to the gentle wind passing through
dreaming to turn into
a white butterfly

Woman of March

the rings of my life tree
show the seasons of my existence
and have the smell of time

having absorbed
nutrients from the dark
winter soil

from the same tree
vernal green leaves emanate
in March light

my eyes begin to see
the transience of life
clouds drift, water flows

no time to be lost
to lament or repent
to forgive or be forgiven

accepting
being human is
beautifully flawed

embracing all in one
with compassion
I march on

This brush writing is the cursive version
of the kanji 慈. It means compassion.
Brush Art Work by Yumiko Tsumura.

Yumiko Tsumura's translation works in collaboration with Samuel Grolmes include:

<u>New Directions Annuals (International Anthology of Prose and Poetry)</u>

New Directions 22   1970 Ryuichi Tamura a long poem
                    "The World Without Words"
New Directions 24   1972 Yumiko Kurahashi short story
                    "The Ugly Devils"
New Directions 26   1973 in memorium Ezra Pound 1885-1972
                    Yumiko Kurahashi short story "Partei"
New Directions 29   1974 Yumiko Kurahashi short story
                    "The Boy who became an Eagle"
<u>New Directions Books</u>

New Directions   2002 Kazuko Shiraishi *Let Those Who Appear*
New Directions   2009 Kazuko Shiraishi *My Floating Mother, City*

<u>Other Publications</u>

CCC Books   1998 Poetry of Ryuichi Tamura
CCC Books   2000 Tamura Ryuichi Poems 1946 -1998
Manoa   2001 Tamura Ryuichi a poem
                    "Four Thousand Days and Night"

Yumiko Tsumura's translation works:

<u>Journals</u>

Manoa   2010 Kazuko Shiraishi, Essay
                    "Landscape of Poetry: Ryuichi Tamura"
New Directions
Exclusive blog   2011 Kazuko Shraishi, a long poem
                    "Sea, Land, Shadow"
                    (March 11, 2011 Tsunami poem)

Two Line	2013	Kazuko Shiraishi, a poem
		"A requiem for the Earth"

St. Petersburg Review 6

2013   Kazuko Shiraishi, poems
"The Bird with Chuvash Language"
"The I heard the Song of the Honey Bee"

Bitter Oleander Press

2014   Kauko Shiraishi, a poem
"Lizard God or Urururu"

Kyoto Journal 80

2014   Kazuko Shiraishi, a long poem
"A Vernal Planet"

Poetry Kanto

2015   Kazuko Shiraishi, poems
"Falling Off the Globe" "Crossing Through"
"The Star" "Ear" "Window of the Eye"

Asymeptote

2016   Kazuko Shiraishi, poems
"By the Hudson River"
"Bird" "A Person dies"

Eastlit

2016   Kazuko Shiraishi poems
"Mischievous God' Birthday"
"The Running of the Full Moon"
"A Spell of Dry Weather"
"March or a Before Dinner Drink"
"In September" "The Crocodiles"
"October Sentimental Journey"

Eleven Eleven   2016   "Yellow Sand"

<u>Book</u>

New Directions   2017   Kazuko Shiraishi *Sea, Land, Shadow*

Yumiko Tsumura was born and raised in the village of Takara by the Pacific Ocean on the Hidaka Plain, in Wakayama Prefecture on the Kii Penishula. She is a graduate of Kwansei Gakuin University with a BA and MA in literature. She has taught American Literature at Baika Women's College in Osaka, and Japanese language, culture and *Shodo* brush writing at colleges in the SF Bay area. She has an MFA in poetry and translation from the University of Iowa Writers workshop. Her poems have appeared in anthologies and journals, including *Kyoto Journal, Kanto Poetry, Eastlit, Manoa* and *Wisconsin Review*. Her book of early poems *The Green Scream* was published by Quixote Press. *Woman of March* is a book of her selected poems, a spiritual snapshots of her path.

She has been a translator of modern Japanese poetry and prose. Her books of translation with Samuel Grolmes include *Tamura Ryuichi Poems 1946 -1998* (CCC Books), Kazuko Shiraishi's *Let Those Who Appear* and *My Floating Mother*, City (New Directions). Her translation of the collected poems of Kazuko Shiraishi *Sea, Land, Shadow* is forthcoming from New Directions in 2017.

She has been a longtime member of the American Literary Translators Association (ALTA) and has contributed in the field of modern Japanese literature. She lives in Palo Alto, California.

www.ingramcontent.com/pod-product-compliance
Lightning Source LLC
Chambersburg PA
CBHW021200090426
42740CB00008B/1163